EVERLASTING ILLUSTRATED CLASSICS

DAVID COPPERFIELD

by
Charles Dickens

Original Novel abridged for
Modern Readers

LITTLE SCHOLARZ PVT LTD.
INDIA

This edition first originated and published in 2019

LITTLE SCHOLARZ Pᴠᴛ Lᴛᴅ.

12-H, New Daryaganj Road, Opp. Officers' Mess, New Delhi-110002 (India)
Phone # 91-11-23275124, 23275224, 23245124, 23261567
email : info@littlescholarz.com
website : www.littlescholarz.com
for online purchase : www.rameshpublishinghouse.com

© LITTLE SCHOLARZ Pᴠᴛ. Lᴛᴅ.

DAVID COPPERFIELD

ISBN: 978-93-86063-45-8

HSN Code: 49011010

Book Code: S-435

Contents

1
I am Born

I was born on a Friday, at twelve o'clock at night. I was born at Blunderstone, in Suffolk, in Scotland. I was a posthumous child.

An aunt of my father's, Miss Trotwood, or Miss Betsey, was the principal magnate of our family. She took her maiden name again, and went to live a long way off.

My father had once been a favourite of her, I beliveve; but she was mortally affronted by his marriage, on the ground that my mother was 'a wax doll'. She had never seen my mother, but she knew her to be not yet twenty.

My father and Miss Betsey never met again. He was double my mother's age when he married, and of but a delicate constitution. He died a year afterwards, and, as I have said, six months before I came into the world.

*My mother was sitting by the fire, when she saw
Miss Betsey coming up the garden.*

This was the state of matters, on the afternoon of, what I may be excused for calling,
that eventful and important Friday.

My mother was sitting by the fire, when
she saw Miss Betsey, coming up the garden.
My mother bent her head, and begged her to
walk in. They went into the parlour.

When My father bought the house, he liked to think that there were rooks about it. So it was called Rookery.

Then Miss Betsey said, 'I have no doubt it will be a girl."

'Perhaps boy,' said my mother.

'We were very happy,' said my mother. 'Mr. Copperfield was only too good to me.'

'Well!' said Miss Betsey. 'You were not equally matched, You were an orphan, And a governess?' weren't you?'

'Yes.'

'David had bought an annuity for himself with his money, I know,' said she, 'What did he do for you?'

'Mr. Copperfield,' said my mother, 'was so considerate and good as to secure the reversion of a part of it to me.'

Meanwhile, Peggotty, coming in and seeing how ill she was,—conveyed her upstairs and immediately dispatched Ham Peggotty, her nephew, to fetch the nurse and doctor.

As the doctor declared that a boy was born to my mother, my aunt vanished like a discontented fairy; and she never came back any more. ꔘꔘꔘ

2
I Observe

The first objects that assume a distinct presence before me, are my mother with her pretty hair and youthful shape, and Peggotty with no shape but dark eyes and cheeks and red hard arms.

I remember the touch of Peggotty's forefinger as she used to hold it out to me, and of its being roughened by needlework.

Among the other things that I remember out of my infancy, are Peggotty's kitchen, on the ground-floor. Then there are the two parlours: the parlour in which we sit of an evening, my mother and I and Peggotty—and the best parlour where we sit on a Sunday.

I remember vividly the churchyard; and our pew in the church.

Peggotty seemed to me a very handsome woman.

After talking a lot about the crocodiles, we had begun with the alligators. When the garden-bell rang, we went out to the door; and there was my mother, and with her a gentleman with beautiful black hair and whiskers.

He patted me on the head; but somehow, I didn't like him or his deep voice. Then my mother started singing and sleep overtook me.

As I woke up I found Peggotty and my mother both in tears, and both talking. There were a lot of arguments between my mother and Peggotty. I feel that Peggotty had hurt my mother's heart.

Thereafter one Sunday, the gentleman was, in church, and he walked home with us.

Gradually, I became used to seeing the gentleman with the black whiskers. I liked him no better than at first, but one autumn morning I was with my mother in the front garden, when Mr. Murdstone—I knew him by that name now—came by, on horseback. He reined up his horse to salute my mother, and offered to take me for a ride.

Mr. Murdstone and I were soon off.

We went to an hotel by the sea, where two gentlemen were smoking cigars in a room by themselves. They were jolly fellows who long had laughed heartily at the joke about Brooks of Sheffield. The names of gentlemen were Quinion and Passindge.

About two months afterwards, Peggotty said, 'Master Davy, how should you like to go along with me and spend a fortnight at my brother's at Yarmouth?

I was flushed by her offer and replied that it would indeed be a treat.

The day soon came for our going. We were to go in a carrier's cart, which departed in the morning after breakfast.

I am glad to recollect that when the carrier's cart was at the gate, and my mother stood there kissing me.

And when the carrier began to move, my mother ran out at the gate, and called to him to stop, that she might kiss me once more.

As we left her standing in the road, Mr. Murdstone came up to where she was, and seemed to expostulate with her for being so moved.

᠆᠆᠆

3
I Have a Change

As we reached Yarmouth, Ham received us. Ham was carrying me on his back. At last we came out upon the dull waste when Ham said, 'Yon's our house, Mas'r Davy!'

Then I learnt that it was a boat.

It was beautifully clean inside. There was a table, and a Dutch clock, and a chest of drawers.

Then Peggotty opened a little door and showed me my bedroom. It was the completest and most desirable bedroom ever seen—in the stern of the vessel; with a little window, where the rudder used to go through.

We were welcomed by a very civil woman in a white apron. After dinner we met Mr. Peggotty, Peggotty's brother and master of the home.

After tea, when the door was shut and all was made snug, it seemed to me the most delicious retreat that the imagination of man

Then Peggotty opened a little door and showed me my bedroom.

could conceive. Little Em'ly had overcome her shyness, and was sitting by my side upon the lowest and least of the lockers, which was just large enough for us two.

Then in a conversation with Mr. Peggotty I learnt that Ham was the son of his brother

Mr. Joe who was also drowned. I also learnt that Mr. Peggotty was a bachelor and the woman in apron was Mrs. Gummidge, the widow of his partner.

Then, later, Peggotty informed me that Ham and Em'ly were an orphan nephew and niece, whom he had adopted in childhood, when they were left destitute.

I was very sensible of my entertainer's goodness, and listened to the women's going to bed in another little crib like mine at the opposite end of the boat.

In the morning I was out with little Em'ly, picking up stones upon the beach. I was surprised when Em'ly told me 'I'm afraid of the sea.'

She called Mr. Peggotty 'Uncle Dam'.

Of course I was in love with little Em'ly. I am sure my love was true and pure. I soon found out that Mrs. Gummidge's was rather a fretful disposition.

At last the day came for my going home. I bore up against the separation from Mr. Peggotty and Mrs. Gummidge, but my agony of mind at leaving little Em'ly was piercing.

As Blunderstone Rookery came, the door opened, and I looked, for my mother, but it was not she, but a strange servant.

'Why, Peggotty!' I said, ruefully, 'isn't she come home?'

'Yes, yes, Master Davy,' said Peggotty. 'She's come home. Wait a bit, Master Davy, and I'll— I'll tell you something.

'Master Davy,' said Peggotty, 'What do you think? You have got a Pa!'

I trembled, and turned white.

Then we went straight to the best parlour, where she left me. On one side of the fire, sat my mother; on the other, Mr. Murdstone.

'Now Clara my dear,' said Mr. Murdstone. 'Recollect! Control yourself, always control yourself! Davy boy, how do you do?'

As soon as I could creep away, I crept upstairs. My old dear bedroom was changed, and I was to lie a long way off and roamed into the yard. I very soon started back from there, for the empty dog-kennel was filled up with a great deep mouthed, black-haired dog— who sprang out to get at me.

4

I Fall into Disgrace

In my new room, with cracks in the ceiling, and flaws in the window-glass. I was crying all the time.

'David,' said, Mr. Murdstone to me, 'if I have an obstinate horse or dog to deal with, what do you think I do? I beat him, you know?'

He seemed to be very fond of my mother—and she was very fond of him. I gathered from what they said, that an elder sister of his was coming to stay with them, for ever and that she was expected that evening.

It was Miss Murdstone who was arrived, and a gloomy-looking lady she was; dark, like her brother. As she looked at me, she said: 'Generally speaking,' 'I don't like boys.' She disposed of me in two words:

'Wants manner!' On the very first morning after her arrival she was up and said:

*I caught the hand with which he held me
in my mouth, and bit it through.*

'Now, Clara, my dear, If you'll be so good as give me your keys, I'll attend to all sort of things in future.' From that time, Miss Murdstone kept the keys with her.

Firmness, I may observe, was the grand quality on which both Mr. and Miss Murdstone took their stand.

There had been some talk on occasions of my going to boarding-school. Mr. and Miss Murdstone had originated it, and my mother had of course agreed with them. In the meantime, I learnt lessons at home.

Shall I ever forget those lessons! They were presided over nominally by my mother, but really by Mr. Murdstone and his sister, who were always present, and found them a favourable occasion for giving my mother lessons in that miscalled firmness.

The natural result of this treatment, which continued, for some six months or more, was to make me sullen, dull, and dogged, and more after, I was shut out from my mother.

However, fortunately, my father had left a small collection of books in a little room up-stairs, to which I had access.

One day as I forgot my lesson, Mr. Murdstone took me into my room, and had my head as in a vice. He cut me heavily an instant afterwards, and in the same instant I caught the hand with which he held me in my mouth, between my teeth, and bit it through.

He beat me then, as if he would have beaten me to death. Then he was gone; and the door was locked outside.

One day I asked Peggotty, 'What is going to be done with me?"

'School. Near London, Tomorrow.' was Peggotty's answer.

In the morning Miss Murdstone appeared as usual, and told me I was going to school. I found my mother, very pale and with red eyes: into whose arms I ran, and begged her pardon from my suffering soul.

'Oh, Davy!' she said. 'That you could hurt anyone I love! Try to be better, pray to be better! I forgive you; but I am so grieved,'

They had persuaded her that I was a wicked fellow, and she was more sorry for that than for my going away. I felt it sorely.

Said my mother. 'Good-bye, Davy. You are going for your own good. Good-bye, my child. You will come home in the holidays, and be a better boy.'

ㄱㄱㄱ

5

I Am Sent Away from Home

We might have gone about half a mile, when I saw, to MY amazement, Peggotty burst from a hedge and climb into the cart. She gave me some cakes and a purse and went away.

At my leisure I examined the purse. It had three bright shillings in it, and two half-crowns folded together in a bit of paper, on which was written, in my mother's hand, 'For Davy. With my love.' I was greatly overcome by this. The name of the carrier was Mr. Barkis. I offered him a cake and told him that Peggotty made it.

He said to me, 'Well! If you was writin' to her, p'raps you'd recollect to say that Barkis was willin'; would you?'

That every evening I wrote a note to Peggotty saying—BARKIS IS WILLING.'

'TAKE CARE OF HIM. HE BITES.'

The coachman had taken me to Yarmouth from where we were to go to London.

What an amazing place London was to me when I saw it in the distance. We approached it by degrees, and got, in due time, to the inn for which we were bound.

From there I was taken by a gaunt, sallow young man, with hollow cheeks, and a chin almost as black as Mr. Murdstone's; 'You're the new boy?' he said. 'Yes, sir,' I said.

'I'm one of the masters at Salem House,' he said. I made him a bow. 'We shall go by the stage-coach. It's about six miles.' he said.

Salem House was enclosed with a high brick wall, and looked very dull. It was a square brick building with wings; of a bare and unfurnished appearance.

It was holiday-time. All the boys were at their several homes. Mr. Creakle, the proprietor, was down by the sea-side with Mrs. and Miss Creakle; I was sent in holiday-time as a punishment for my misdoing, all of which he explained to me as we went along.

I gazed upon the schoolroom into which he took me, as the most forlorn and desolate place I had ever seen.

Mr. Mell having left me there, I came upon a pasteboard placard, beautifully written, which was lying on the desk, and bore these words: 'TAKE CARE OF HIM. HE BITES.'

At first, I thought it was for some dog, undereath a desk, but as Mr. Mell came, he told me, 'No, Copperfield,' 'that's not a dog. That's a boy. My instructions are, Copperfield, to put this placard on your back.

I am sorry to make such a beginning with you, but I must do it.' With that he took me down, and tied the placard, on my shoulders like a knapsack; and wherever I went, afterwards, I had to carry it.

What I suffered from that placard, nobody can imagine. I had not much noticed that it was a man with a wooden leg who had opened the gate.

From the inscriptions I could read certain names, among them, J. Steerforth, Tommy Traddles, and George Demple, who I fancied would make fun of me—and there were five-and-forty of them in the school then.

Mr. Mell never said much to me, but he was never harsh to me. I suppose we were company to each other, without talking.

6
I Enlarge My Circle of Acquaintance

One day I was called by Mr. Creakle. He, pinched my ear with ferocious playfulness.

I'll tell you what I am,' whispered Mr. Creakle. 'I am a determined character, I do my duty.'

Next morning Mr. Sharp came back. Mr. Sharp was the first master, and superior to Mr. Mell.

The first boy who returned and became friendly to me was Tommy Traddles. I learnt that I belonged to his bedroom. He being senior to me, he kept my money safe.

He introduced me to other boys. I heard that the man with the wooden leg, whose name was Tungay, had formerly assisted Creakle in the hop business, having done a deal of dishonest work for him.

However, Mr. Creakle never laid a hand, on a boy, J. Steerforth. ❑❑❑

7

My 'First Half' at Salem House

School began in earnest next day. I remember, by the roar of voices in the schoolroom suddenly becoming hushed as death when Mr. Creakle entered after breakfast. After a dreadful exordium he showed me the cane, and asked me what I thought of that?

He was very honourable, Traddles was, and held it as a solemn duty in the boys to stand by one another. He suffered for this on several occasions. Mr. Sharp and Mr. Mell were both notable personages in my eyes.

Steerforth continued his protection of me, and proved a very useful friend.

One Saturday both Mr. Creakle and Mr. Sharp were out. Mr. Mell was teaching.

There was a noisy exchange of hot words between Mr. Mell and Steerforth. Then suddenly Mr. Creakle came. After an analysis of the situation, Steerforth was considered a hero. Mr. Mell left his job in a huff. Poor Mr. Mell!

One afternoon, Mr. Peggotty and Ham, came. We shook hands in a very cordial way; and I laughed and laughed, and then we all three laughed.

After conveying me news about different members at home they laid before me a file of two prodigious lobsters, and an enormous crab.

I could not help asking about Em'ly.

'She's getting to be a woman, that's wot she's getting to be,' said Mr. Peggotty.

Then suddenly Steerforth popped in. Mr. Peggotty and Ham invited Steerforth to visit their home.

The rest of the half-year is a jumble in my recollection of the daily strife and struggle of our lives.

I well remember though, how the distant idea of the holidays, began to come towards us, and to grow and grow.

How from counting months, we came to weeks, and then to days; I was thinking about all these old things when I was inside the carrier.

8

My Holidays, Especially One Happy Afternoon

When I returned from school after holidays Mr. Barkis again was the carrier.

'I gave your message, Mr. Barkis,' I said: 'I wrote to Peggotty.'

'You might tell her, if you would,' said Mr. Barkis, 'that Barkis was a-waitin' for a answer. Says you—what name is it?'

'Her name is Peggotty and her Christian name is Clara.'

The carrier put my box down at the garden-gate, and left me. It seemed that Mr. and Miss Murdstone had gone out upon a visit in the neighbourhood, and would not return before night. We dined together by the fireside.

When I told Peggotty about Mr. Barkis, she cried, 'Oh!, 'he wants to marry me.'

'It would be a very good match for you; wouldn't it?' said my mother.

'Oh! I don't know,' said Peggotty.

It was almost ten o'clock when Mr. and Miss Murdstone came. I went upstairs at once.

Early in the morning I begged pardon of Mr. Murdstone. 'I am glad to hear you are sorry, David,' he replied.

'I was sorry, David,' said Mr. Murdstone, 'to observe that you are of a sullen disposition.'

'I beg your pardon, sir,' I faltered. 'I have never meant to be sullen since I came back.'

'Don't take refuge in a lie, sir!' he returned fiercely, 'You have withdrawn yourself in your sullenness to your own room. You know now, once for all, that I require you to be here, and not there. Sit down.'

'One thing more,' he said, 'I observe that you have an attach-ment to low and common company. You are not to associate with servants.' Then, he asked my mother also not to give respect to Peggotty.

As the holidays came to an end, I was not sorry to go. Again Mr. Barkis appeared at the gate. I kissed my mother, and my baby brother, and went away.

9

I Have a Memorable Birthday

The anniversary of my birthday came round in March. There was a gap of full two months between my return to Salem House and the arrival of that birthday.

How well I recollect the kind of day it was! It was after breakfast, when Mr. Sharp entered and said: 'David Copperfield is to go into the parlour.'

I hurried away to the parlour, and there I found Mr. Creakle, and Mrs. Creakle with an opened letter in her hand.

I learnt from them that my mother was dead. I thought of my mother and so many things like my home, my father, grave in the churchyard and o.....

I thought of the little baby, who, Mrs. Creakle said, had been pining away for some time, and who, they believed, would die too.

We went into a little parlour behind the shop.

I left Salem House upon the morrow afternoon. I little thought then that I left it, never to return. We did not get into Yarmouth before ten o'clock in the morning. I looked out for Mr. Barkis, but instead of him a fat, little old man in black, came to take me home.

We walked away to a shop in a narrow street, on which was written OMER, DRAPER, TAILOR, HABERDASHER, FUNERAL FUR-NISHER, &c. We went into a little back-parlour behind the shop, where we found three young women at work on a quantity of black materials.

'Do you know how my little brother is, sir?' I inquired. 'Don't mind it more than you can help,' said Mr. Omer. 'Yes. The baby's dead.'

The chaise soon came round to the front of the shop, and the baskets being put in first, I was put in next, and those three followed.

I was in Peggotty's arms before I got to the door, and she took me into the house. Mr. Murdstone took no head of me.

At the funeral, there were many faces that I knew, among the little crowd; but I don't need to mention any.

Peggotty came to me and told me in detail about the illness of my mother.

The mother who lay in the grave, was the mother of my infancy; the little creature in her arms, was myself, as I had once been, hushed for ever on her bosom.

10

I Become Neglected, and Am Provided for

Peggotty said to me, 'I'm a-going, Davy,— you see, to my brother's, for another fortnight's visit—perhaps, as they don't want you here you might go along with me.' I weighed the offer and accepted it despite Miss Murdstone's opposition to it.

Mr. Barkis came into the house for Peggotty's boxes. I had never known him to pass the garden-gate before, but on this occasion he came into the house. And he shouldered the largest box and went out.

Peggotty was naturally in low spirits at leaving what had been her home so many years. When she came to herself, Mr. Barkis, slid nearer to her on the seat, and nudged her with his elbow.

Mr. Peggotty and Ham waited for us at the old place. They received me and Peggotty in an affectionate manner, and shook hands with Mr. Barkis, who, had a shame-faced leer upon his countenance.

When Peggotty told me that she was thinking marrying Barkis, I said, 'It would be a very good thing.'

'Barkis is a good plain creature,' said Peggotty.

When we came to Mr. Peggotty's cottage we saw that there was no little Em'ly to be seen. So I asked Mr. Peggotty where she was.

'She's at school, sir,' said Mr. Peggotty.

Shortly afterwords, Em'ly came, but she didn't care a bit. She saw me well enough; but instead of turning round and calling after me, ran away laughing.

She seemed to delight in teasing me, which was a change in her I wondered at very much.

Little Em'ly and I seldom wandered on the beach now. She had tasks to learn, and needle-work to do; and was absent during a great part of each day. She was more of a little woman than I had supposed.

On the very first evening after our arrival, Mr. Barkis appeared with a bundle of oranges tied up in a handkerchief. After that occasion he appeared every evening at exactly the same hour, and always with a little bundle.

Sometimes he took Peggotty out for a walk on the flats, After he was gone, Peggotty would throw her apron over her face, and laugh for half-an-hour.

When the term of my visit was nearly expired, it was given out that Peggotty and Mr. Barkis were going to make a day's holiday together, and that little Em'ly and I were to accompany them. While we were yet at break-fast, Mr. Barkis appeared in the distance, driving a chaise-cart towards the object of his affections.

Away we went, on our holiday excursion; and the first thing we did was to stop at a church, where Mr. Barkis tied the horse to some rails, and went in with Peggotty, leaving little Em'ly and me alone in the chaise. I took that occasion to put my arm round Em'ly's waist, and propose that as I was going away so very soon now, we should determine to be very affectionate to one another, and very happy, all day. Little Em'ly consented, and allowed me to kiss her.

Mr. Barkis and Peggotty were a good while in the church, but came out at last. Clara Peggotty was Clara Peggotty BARKIS! now.

In a word, they were married.

Well, we came to the old boat again in good time at night; and there Mr. and Mrs. Barkis bade us good-bye, and drove away snugly to their own home. I felt then, for the first time, that I had lost Peggotty.

Then I took leave of Mr. Peggotty, and Ham, and Mrs. Gummidge, and little Em'ly, that day; and passed the night at Peggotty's, in a little room in the roof (with the Crocodile Book on a shelf by the bed's head) which was to be always mine, Peggotty said, and should always be kept for me in exactly the same state.

I was going home in the morning, and I went home in the morning, with Peggotty and Mr. Barkis in the cart. They left me at the gate, and it was a strange sight to me to see the cart go on, taking Peggotty away, leaving me behind. I was not beaten, or starved; I was coldly neglected.

At all times I lounged about the house and neighbourhood quite disregarded, except that they were jealous of my making any friends, and I was seldom allowed to visit Peggotty.

One day Mr. Murdstone said to me,' you know, David, that I am not rich. You have received some considerable education already. What is before you now, is a fight with the world; and the sooner you begin it, the better.'

'You have heard' he continued, 'the "counting-house" mentioned sometimes, of Murdstone and Grinby, in the wine trade.'

'Mr. Quinion manages that business.'

'Mr. Quinion suggests that it gives employment to some other boys, and that he sees no reason why it shouldn't, on the same terms, give employment to you.'

'Those terms are, that you will earn enough for yourself to provide for your eating and drinking, and pocket-money. Your lodging (which I have arranged for) will be paid by me. So will your washing—'

So, the next morning I left in the post-chaise Mr. Quinion to the London coach at Yarmouth!

◗◗◗

11

I Begin Life on My Own Account, and Don't Like it

So I became, at ten years old, a little labouring hand in the service of Murdstone and Grinby.

Murdstone and Grinby's warehouse was at the waterside. Murdstone and Grinby's trade was among a good many kinds of people, but an important branch of it was the supply of wines and spirits to certain packet ships.

There were three or four of us, counting me. My working place was established in a corner of the warehouse, where Mr. Quinion could see me. Then Mr. Quinion introduced me to a stoutish, middle-aged person.

'This is Mr. Micawber,' said Mr. Quinion to me. He is known to Mr. Murdstone. He takes orders for us on commission. He has been written to by Mr. Murdstone, on the subject of your lodgings, and he will receive you as a lodger.'

Mr. Quinion introduced me to a stoutish, middle-aged man.

He talked to me in a very friendly way and offered to take me to his house at eight that day in the evening.

At the appointed time in the evening, Mr. Micawber and I walked to his house. He presented me to Mrs. Micawber, a thin and faded lady, not at all young, who was sitting in the parlour with a baby at her breast.

A dark-complexioned young woman, who was servant to the family, informed me, that she was 'a Orfling', and came from St. Luke's workhouse, in the neighbourhood. My room was at the top of the house, at the back.

I learnt from Mrs Micawber that Mr. Micawber was passing through great difficulties as he was deeply in debt.

In order to pay their debts, the Micawbers had to dispose of their house articles including the few books they had. Mrs. Micawber begged to make use of me to any extent. I began to dispose of the more portable articles of property that very evening.

At last Mr. Micawber was arrested early one morning for debts and carried over to the King's Bench Prison in the Borough.

Mr. Micawber's affairs, although past their crisis, were very much involved by reason of a certain 'Deed'.

Mrs. Micawber informed me that 'her family' had decided that Mr. Micawber should apply for his release under the Insolvent

Debtors Act, which would set him free, she expected, in about six weeks.

I call to mind that Mr. Micawber, about this time, composed a petition to the House of Commons, praying for an alteration in the law of imprisonment for debt.

There was a club in the prison, in which Mr. Micawber, as a gentleman, was a great authority. Mr. Micawber had stated his idea of this petition to the club, and the club had strongly approved of the same, wherefore Mr. Micawber had set a time for all the members of the club to come up to his room and sign it.

❏❏❏

12

Liking Life on My Own Account No Better, I Form a Great Resolution

In due time, Mr. Micawber's petition was ripe for hearing; and that gentleman was ordered to be discharged under the Act. Then Mrs. Micawber told me about his papa and mama, and how her papa had helped Mr. Micawber several times.

Then she said, 'my family are of opinion that Mr. Micawber should quit London, and exert his talents in the country.' Mr. Micawber is a man of great talent, Master Copperfield.

'Something might be done for a man of his ability in the Custom House. The influence of my family being local, it is their wish that Mr. Micawber should go down to Plymouth.'

As for herself she said, 'I never will desert Mr. Micawber.' She repeated these words several times after short intervals. Mrs. Micawber seemed to be alarmingly in the lowest spirits. Mr. Quinion arranged a rented accommodation for Mr. Micawber.

Then Mr. Micawber gave me a number of pieces of advice for peace and happiness.

But with no intention of passing many more weary days there. No. I had resolved to run away. To go, by some means or other, down into the country, to the only relation I had in the world, and tell my story to my aunt, Miss Betsey.

As I did not know where Miss Betsey lived, I wrote a long letter to Peggotty and asked her, I also mentioned my need for money. She sent me half a guinea. Besides, I learnt from her that Betsey lived near Dover.

A great difficulty arose for me when a long-legged young man with a very little empty donkey-cart ran away on his cart with my half a guniea box.

I ran after him as fast as I could, but I had no breath to call out with. I narrowly escaped being run over, twenty times at least, in half a mile.

At length, I left the young man to go where he would with my box and money; and, panting and crying, but never stopping, faced about for Greenwich, which I had understood was on the Dover Road. ❏❏❏

13

The Sequel of My Resolution

While going towards Greenwich I happened to pass a little shop, where it was written up that ladies' and gentlemen's wardrobes were bought. There I sold my waistcoat, for nine pence. I foresaw pretty clearly that my jacket would go next.

A plan had occurred to me for passing the night. I came to Salem House; and I found a haystack in the corner, and I lay down by it.

In the morning, I struck on the Dover Road.

Feeling that I could go but a very little way that day, I sold off my jacket for four pence. But at an expense of three pence I soon refreshed myself completely.

As I came near Dover, I inquired about my aunt. At last I reached a shop where I met MY aunt's handmaid, who led me to her.

My shoes, my hat, my shirt and trousers and hair were all by this time in a woeful condition.

As I saw Miss Betsey, I said, 'I am your nephew, I am David Copperfield, of Blunderstone, in Suffolk,—where you came, on the night when I was born, and saw my dear mama. I have been very unhappy since she died.'

She took me into the parlour and called her servant, Janet, who fetched Dick, a florid, pleasant looking gentleman, with a grey head. She told about him and about my father. On Mr. Dick's suggestion first of all, I was given a hot bath.

After dinner, she began to talk about my mother, and said, 'Whatever possessed that poor Baby, to go and be married again?'

Then she began to talk about Peggotty.

But I told her that Peggotty was the best, the truest, the most faithful, most devoted, and most self-denying friend and servant in the world; who had ever loved me dearly, and who had ever loved my mother dearly.

Then I was put to bed. Soon I was absorbed into the world of dreams.　❑❑❑

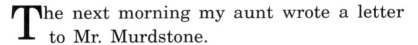

14

My Aunt Makes up Her Mind About Me

The next morning my aunt wrote a letter to Mr. Murdstone.

Then she told me about Dick. 'Mr. Richard Babley—that's the gentleman's true name.' said she. Then she told me about Dick's history and about his sister, who was made wretched by her husband.

I must say that the generosity of her championship of poor harmless Mr. Dick, not only inspired my young breast with some selfish hope for myself, but warmed it unselfishly towards her.

Mr. Murdstone replied, that he was coming to speak to her himself on the next day. It was late at night she gave a sudden alarm of donkeys. I beheld Miss Murdstone, on a side-saddle, ride deliberately over the sacred piece of green, and stop in front of the house.

I beheld Miss Mudrstone ride over the sacred piece of green.

My aunt said, 'Go away! Janet, turn them round. Lead them off!' Miss Murdstone had by now dismounted, and soon I saw Mr. and Miss Murdstone enter the room.

Dick was called for whom my aunt described as 'An old and intimate friend, on whose judgement, I rely.'

Mr. Murdstone expressed grave doubts about my disposition, temper and capacity to work or make or keep friends.

My aunt tried to clear the air against me all along and even talked about my right to annuity after my mother's death.

At last Murdstone said, 'I am not here to take David back unconditionally, but to dispose of him as I think proper.' He charged my aunt of abetting me, and he warned her not to come between him and me. 'I am here, for the first and last time, to take him away.'

'And what does the boy say?' said my aunt. 'Are you ready to go, David?'

I answered no, and entreated her not to let me go.

Then my aunt said to Mr. Murdstone:

'You can go when you like; I'll take my chance with the boy. If he's all you say he is, at least I can do as much for him then, as you have done. But I don't believe a word of it.'

'Good day, sir,' said my aunt, 'and good-bye! Good day to you, too, ma'am,' said my aunt.

15

I Make Another Beginning

$\mathbf{M}$r. Dick and I soon became the best of friends. Every day of his life he had a long sitting at the Memorial, which never made the least progress, for King Charles the First always strayed into it, sooner or later.

'Trot,' said my aunt one evening, 'we must not forget your education.'

I was taken by her to Mr. Wickfield, the lawyer's office. There first we met Uriah Heep. 'This is my grand-nephew,' said my aunt to Mr. Wickfield, 'I have brought him here, to put him to a school where he may be thoroughly well taught, and well treated.' Then said Mr. Wickfield : 'Leave your nephew here, for the present.'

We accordingly went up a wonderful old staircase; A girl of about my own age came quickly. I learnt Agnes Wickfield was the girl's name. ❏❏❏

16

I Am a New Boy in More Senses than One

Next morning, I was taken by Mr. Wickfield, to a new school—and was introduced to my new master, Doctor Strong.

Sitting at work, not far from Doctor Strong, was Annie, his pretty young wife.

About five-and-twenty boys were studiously engaged at their books when we went in.

I felt easier at Wickfield's than in school. Agnes was in the drawing-room. She met me with her pleasant smile, and we had some hearty talk.

'Mama has been dead ever since I was born,' she said, in her quiet way. Meanwhile Mr. Wickfield came. According to Agnes, Mr. Wickfield was the least suspicious of mankind.

Then, I found Uriah reading a great fat book.

'I am not doing office-work, Master Copper-field,' said Uriah. 'I am improving my legal knowledge,'

'I suppose you are quite a great lawyer?' I said, after looking at him for some time.

'Me, Master Copperfield?' said Uriah. 'Oh, no! I'm a very umble person. and so is my mother'.

At school, among other boys, I was awkward enough in their games, and backward enough in their studies.

Accordingly, I went to work very hard, both in play and in earnest, and gained great commendation.

Doctor Strong's was an excellent school; as different from Mr. Creakle's as good is from evil. It was very decorously ordered, and on a sound system; with an appeal, in everything, to the honour and good faith of the boys.

Some of the higher scholars boarded in the Doctor's house, and the doctor himself was a great scholar, having mastered the Greek roots. I learnt that he had married for love.

As for Mrs. Strong, she had taken a liking for me on the morning of my introduction to the Doctor. ◻◻◻

17
Somebody Turns Up

Undoubtedly, Peggotty was a most self-denying friend of mine. I wrote two letters to her while at Dover. To these communications Peggotty replied promptly.

I made out that she could not take quite kindly to my aunt yet. She was evidently still afraid of Miss Betsey.

She gave me one piece of intelligence namely, that there had been a sale of the furniture at our old home, and that Mr. and Miss Murdstone were gone away, and the house was shut up, to be let or sold. Mr. Barkis was an excellent husband, she said.

One day Mr. Dick said to me perhaps there is a man that hides near their house and frightens Miss Betsey to whom she goes and gives money secretly. I thought it to be Dick's delusion.

She received me with the utmost humility

One evening I visited Uriah's on his invitation to tea. His mother received me with the utmost humility saying, 'Umble we are, umble we have been, umble we shall ever be.'

They respectfully catered to me the choicest of the eatables on the table.

Suddenly Mr. Micawber appeared there.

'Walking along the street,' he said, 'I was reflecting upon the probability of something turning up'.

As for Mrs. Micawber, 'She will be rejoiced, Copperfield, to renew her acquaintance with you.' I said I should be delighted to see her.

I could do no less, under these circumstances, than make Mr. Micawber known to Uriah Heep and his mother. Then I told him that I was a pupil at Doctor Strong's. 'I am extremely happy to hear it,' said Mr. Micawber.

'Shall we go and see Mrs. Micawber, sir?' I said, to get Mr. Micawber away.

To this Mr. Micawber said, 'Yes' Then we moved away. It was a little inn where Mr. Micawber put up, and he occupied a little room in it.

Mrs. Micawber was amazed, but very glad to see me. I was very glad to see her too.

I learnt from Mrs. Micawber that Mr. Micawber could not obtain any employment in the custom house. She said, 'Moreover, even the reception from our own members of family at Plymouth was cool.'

When I took my leave of them, they both pressed me so much to come and dine before they went away, that I could not refuse. As I was looking out of window that same evening, it surprised me, to see Mr. Micawber and Uriah Heep walk past, arm in arm: I was still more surprised, when I went to the little hotel next day at the appointed dinner-hour, to find, from what Mr. Micawber said, that he had gone home with Uriah, and had drunk brandy-and-water at Mrs. Heep's.

At seven o'clock next morning, I received the communication, in which Mr. Micawber said that there was no hope of the remittance he gave under these circumstances, which was sure to lead to his destruction. So I must learn a lesson from his circumstances.

I was so shocked by the contents of this heart-rending letter, that I ran off directly towards the little hotel But, half-way there, I met the London coach with Mr. and Mrs. Micawber up behind; Mr. Micawber, the very picture of tranquil enjoyment, smiling at Mrs. Micawber's conversation, eating walnuts out of a paper bag, with a bottle sticking out of his breast pocket.   ❏❏❏

18
A Retrospect

At the age of seventeen I began to develop erotic thoughts. I fell in love with a number of girls or ladies one after the other.

At first, it was one Miss Shepherd of Miss Nettuingalls establishement. I danced with her and gave her nuts, biscuits and oranges, and even kissed her. But she rejected me.

Then I started wearing a gold chain, a ring and a long-tailed coat and used a great deal of bear's greese.

Then one oldest Miss Larkins became the object of my love. I was in a happy dream and I waltzed with her. But I was disappointed when I learnt about her marrying another man.

This, and the resumption of my ring, as well as of the bear's grease in moderation, are the last marks I can discern, now, in my progress to seventeen. ❑❑❑

19

I Look About Me, And Make a Discovery

At last my school-days drew to an end. My aunt and I had held many grave deliberations on the calling to which I should be devoted.

At last she said, 'Go to Peggotty, know your own mind and form a cooler judgement.'

'That you may begin, in a small way, to have a reliance upon yourself, and to act for yourself,' said my aunt, 'I shall send you upon your trip, alone.'

I was shortly afterwards fitted out with a handsome purse of money, and a portmanteau, and tenderly dismissed upon my expedition. I was at liberty to do what I would, for three weeks or a month.

I went to Canterbury first, that I might take leave of Agnes and Mr. Wickfield.

I myself noted and learnt from Agnes that Mr. Wickfield was in a miserable condition.

I saw him, only the other evening, when he lay down his head upon his desk and shed tears like a child.

Then we went to drink tea at the Doctor's, The Doctor was very fond of music. Agnes sang with great sweetness and expression, and so did Mrs. Strong. They sang together, and played duets together, and we had quite a little concert. I noticed that Mr. Wickfield seemed to dislike the intimacy between Annie and Agnes. I too became suspicious of Annie's inner thoughts, especially in regard to Maldon, her cousin while Agnes was a model of innocence.

Morning brought with it my parting from the old house, which Agnes had filled with her influence; as I took my seat upon the box of London coach.

I had visited Juluis Caesar at a theater. When I saw Steerforth before me, I told him about myself and he said, 'Well, I am what they call an Oxford man, and I am on my way now to my mother's.'

An important thing Steerforth did was to get my room changed to a better one, where I had a sound sleep full of happy dreams.

⊐⊐⊐

20
Steerforth's Home

I found Steerforth expecting me, in a snug private apartment. Hearing about all I was doing, he took me home to Highgate. He preferred to call me Daisy.

A handsome face, was in the doorway as we alighted. The lady he presented me as his mother, and she gave me a stately welcome.

There was a second lady in the dining-room. She was introduced as Miss Dartle, and both Steerforth and his mother called her Rosa.

It was amusing to see Miss Dartle speaking such words 'Really?' ' Oh, really? 'Oh! Yes,' etc. so frequently.

It was no matter of wonder to me to find Mrs. Steerforth devoted to her son. She seemed to be able to speak or think about nothing else.

I found a likeness of Miss Dartle looking eagerly at me. ☐☐☐

21
Little Em'ly

There was a servant in that house, a man who, I understood, was usually with Steerforth, and had come into his service at the University.

Littimer was in my room in the morning before I was up to bring me shaving water, and to put out my clothes.

He got horses for us; and Steerforth, who knew everything, gave me lessons in riding. He provided foils for us, and Steerforth gave me lessons in fencing. The week passed away in a most delightful manner.

At, last, we bade adieu to Mrs. Steerforth and Miss Dartle, with many thanks on my part, Littimer's was left at home.

We decided to go to Peggotty's. He stayed there with me to dinner. At eight o'clock we started forth, for Mr. Pegotty's boat.

As Ham holds her by the hand, little Em'ly is blushing and shy.

I laid my hand upon the latch; and whispering Steerforth to keep close to me, went in. We heard, a clapping of hands: which I was surprised to see, proceeded from the generally disconsolate Mrs. Gummidge. But Mrs. Gummidge was not the only person there who was unusually excited.

Ham, held little Em'ly by the hand, as if he were presenting her to Mr. Peggotty; little Em'ly herself, blushing and shy, but delighted with Mr. Peggotty's delight.

'Now you see, our little Em'ly is in a fair way of being married,' said Mr. Peggotty.

Whether I had come there with any lingering fancy that I was still to love little Em'ly, I don't know. I know that I was filled with pleasure by all this.

Presently they brought her to the fireside, very much confused, and very shy,—but she soon became more assured when she found how gently and respectfully Steerforth spoke to her.

It was almost midnight when we took our leave. I saw the sweet blue eyes of little Em'ly peeping after us, from behind Ham, and heard her soft voice calling to us to be careful.

'A most engaging little Beauty!' said Steerforth, taking my arm. 'How fortunate we are, too,' I returned, 'to have arrived to witness their happiness in that intended marriage! I never saw people so happy.'

❏❏❏

22

Some Old Scenes, and Some New People

Steerforth and I stayed for more than a fortnight in that part of the country.

'I have taken a fancy to the place. 'I have bought a boat that was for sale—a clipper—and Mr. Peggotty will be master of her in my absence.'

'Now I understand you, Steerforth!' said I, exultingly. 'You pretend to have bought it for yourself, but you have really done so to confer a benefit on him.'

Suddenly there passed us—a young woman. She was lightly dressed; looked bold, and haggard, and flaunting, and poor.

It was Miss Martha, a beautician of sorts, who moved up and down in town but was generally disregarded by people. As we reached home we found the same girl there. Peggotty had been crying. So had little Em'ly.

'Martha wants,' Em'ly said to Ham, 'to go to London.'

'What will she do there?' inquired Ham.

'I'll try,' said Martha, 'if you'll help me away. I never can do worse than I have done here.'

As Em'ly held out her hand to Ham, I saw him put in it a little canvas bag.

'It's all yourn, Em'ly,' I could hear him say.

The tears rose freshly in her eyes, but she turned away and went to Martha. What she gave her, I don't know. I saw her stooping over her, and putting money in her bosom.

Then Martha arose, and gathering her shawl about her, covering her face with it, and weeping aloud, she went away.

As the door closed, little Em'ly looked at us three in a hurried manner and then hid her face in her hands, and fell to sobbing.

'Oh, Ham!' she exclaimed, still weeping pitifully, 'I am not so good a girl as I ought to be! I know I have not the thankful heart, sometimes, I ought to have!'

'Yes, yes, you have, I'm sure,' said Ham.

⌐⌐⌐

23

I Corroborate Mr. Dick, and Choose a Profession

While we were at breakfast, a letter was delivered to me from my aunt. In it she advised me to think of becoming a proctor.

I quite made up my mind to do so. I then told Steerforth that my aunt was in town awaiting me, and we went to see her.

'Well, Trot,' my aunt began, 'what do you think of the proctor plan?'

I told my aunt that I liked the idea and so did Steerforth.

'However', I further explained, 'my only worry is that it might be very expensive and an extra burden on you when you have already expended a great deal on my education, and have always been extra liberal to me in all things.

'So, I only ask you, my second mother, to consider.'

Doctor's Commons was approached by a little low archway.

'Trot, my child, if I have any object in life, it is to provide for your being a good, a sensible, and a happy man. I am bent upon it—so is Dick.'

Accordingly, she took me to Messrs Spenlow and Jorkins, in Doctors' Commons.

Doctors' Commons was approached by a little low archway.

Mr. Spenlow said, 'I must mention I have a partner, Mr. Jorkins. And Mr. Jorkins is strict in fulfilment of all terms of the bond'.

'And the premium, Stamp included, is a thousand pounds,' said Mr. Spenlow.

It was settled that I should begin my month's probation as soon as I pleased. Then Mr. Spenlow offered to take me into Court then and there.

Mr. Spenlow led me into a large dull room.

Very well satisfied with the dreamy nature of this retreat, I informed Mr. Spenlow that I had seen enough for that time, and we rejoined my aunt; in company with whom I presently departed from the Commons.

As for my dwelling an advertisement directed us to one Mr. Crupp. Accordingly we rung the area bell and had Mr. Crupp before us. So we went upstairs.

My aunt, seeing how enraptured I was with the premises, took them for a month, Mrs. Crupp expressly intimated that she should always yearn towards me as a son. ⊐⊐⊐

24

My First Dissipation

I left the Commons early on the third day, and walked out to Highgate. I had invited Steerforth and his two Oxford friends to have dinner. At dinner, everything was very good; and there was no pause in our festivity.

Steerforth had made a brilliant speech about me, I returned thanks, and hoped the present company would dine with me tomorrow, and the day after—each day.

Shortly afterwards, we were very high up in a very hot theatre, crammed with people.

On somebody's motion, we resolved to go downstairs to the dress-boxes, where the ladies were. I was surprised to see Agnes, sitting on the seat before me. A gentleman was beside her.

She sent me away. I felt ashamed and went away in anger. Later I told Steerforth that Agnes was my sister. ❑❑❑

25
Good and Bad Angels

The next morning I received a letter from Agnes, in which she asked me to come to her that day at Mr. Waterbrookis, where she was staying.

After leaving office I called on her. I called her, 'My good angel.' Then she asked me to beware of 'bad angels.'

Agnes warned me against Steerforth, whom she called 'my bad angel,' but I opposed her opinion strongly.

Then she talked about Uriah Heep and said, 'I believe he is going to enter into partnership with papa.'

'What? Uriah? That mean, fawning fellow!' I cried, 'Agnes! You must not allow your father to take such a mad step, act, while there's time.'

She replied: 'Uriah has made himself indispensable to papa. He has mastered papa's weaknesses, fostered them, and taken advantage of them, until papa is afraid of him.'

She advised me to be friendly to Uriah, 'though he may not deserve it',

Soon, the room door opened, and Mrs. Waterbrook—came sailing in.

I found Uriah Heep among the company, in a suit of black, and in deep humility.

I asked him, if he would come home to my rooms, and have some coffee. 'Oh, really, Master Copperfield,' he rejoined—

Then, he said to me in confidence, 'the image of Miss Agnes has been in my breast for years. Oh, Master Copperfield, with what a pure affection do I love the ground my Agnes walks on!' I believe I had a delirious idea of seizing the red-hot poker out of the fire, and running him through with it. But my remembrance of the entreaty of Agnes, held me back.

'There's no hurry at present, you know, Master Copperfield,' Uriah proceeded, 'My Agnes is very young still; and mother and me will have to work our way upwards, and make a good many new arrangements, before it would be quite convenient.'   ❏❏❏

26

I Fall into Captivity

I was at the coach office to take leave of her and see her go; and there was he, returning to Canterbury by the same conveyance.

However, at the coach window, as at the dinner-party, he hovered about us without a moment's intermission, gorging himself on every syllable that I said to Agnes, or Agnes said to me.

I was articled to Spenlow and Jorkins. I had ninety pounds a year from my aunt. Mr. Spenlow was as good as his word. In a week or two, he referred to this engagement, and said, that if I would do him the favour to come down next Saturday, and stay till Monday, he would be extremely happy.

Of course I said I would do him the favour; and he was to drive me down in his phaeton, and to bring me back.

We were very pleasant, going down, and Mr. Spenlow gave me some hints in reference to my profession. He said it was the genteelest profession in the world, and must on no account be confounded with the profession of a solicitor.

We went into Mr. Spenlow's house, which was cheerfully lighted up. 'Where is Miss Dora?' said Mr. Spenlow to the servant. 'Dora!' I thought. 'What a beautiful name!'

All was over in a moment. I had fulfilled my destiny. I was a captive and a slave. I loved Dora Spenlow to distraction!

Then I learnt that Dora had a confidential friend, Miss Murdstone!

In Mr. Spenlow's house there was a beautiful garden. I was wandering in this garden of Eden all the while, with Dora.

Dora's opinion of Miss Murdstone was this : 'She is a tiresome creature. I can't think what papa can have been about, when he chose such a vexatious thing to be my companion.'

'Papa calls her my confidential friend, but I am sure she is no such thing'.

27

Tommy Traddles

Tommy Traddles was one of my classmates at Salem House. The next day, in the afternoon, I reached his dwelling place.

I could easily recall his good temper, and something of his old unlucky fortune.

He had started the work of copying law writings, and thus he was an average compiler.

'You must know that I am engaged.' 'She is a curate's daughter,' said Traddles; 'one of ten, down in Devonshire. Yes!'

'I don't make much, but I don't spend much,' said he. Mr. Micawber was his landlord. Micawber.

As I met him, Mr. Micawber slightly bowed to me. I learnt that he was now engaged in the sale of corn upon commission though not with much success.

ㄱㄱㄱ

28

Mr. Micawber's Gauntlet

I had given dinner to Steerforth and his Oxford friends. Now, I decided to entertain my newly formed old friends. At the appointed time, my visitors arrived together, Mr. Micawber and Traddles. They were all delighted with my residence and highly satisfied with the feast.

'The articles of corn and coals,' said Mrs. Micawber, still more argumentatively, 'being equally out of the question, Mr. Copperfield, I naturally look round the world, and say, "What is there in which a person of Mr. Micawber's talent is likely to succeed?" And I exclude the doing anything on commission, because commission is not a certainty.

'I will not conceal from you, my dear Mr. Copperfield,' said Mrs. Micawber, 'that I have long felt the Brewing business to be particularly adapted to Mr. Micawber.

Mrs. Micawber said that Mr. Micawber in spite of being highly talented, had failed. So, he had decided to throw down the gauntlet to society by advertising.

'Advertising is rather expensive,' I remarked. 'Exactly so!' said Mrs. Micawber, 'It is for that reason especially, that I think Mr. Micawber ought to raise a certain sum of money—on a bill, which can be discounted in the money market, if necessary. I view it, steadily, as an investment. which is sure of return.'

Then Traddles said, 'I have come from Yarmouth.'

'And how are they all? Of course, little Emily is not married yet?' I asked.

'Not yet. Going to be, I believe—in so many weeks, or months, or something or other. 'I have a letter for you from Peggotty.' It informed me of her husband's hopeless state.

Later, I had a letter from Mr. Micawber.

Micawber mentioned how he and Traddles had been put to great inconvience by an individual, who had taken legal possession of their chattels. All this greatfully worried me.

29

I Visit Steerforth at His Home, Again

I mentioned to Mr. Spenlow in the morning, that I wanted leave of absence for a short time.

Mrs. Steerforth was pleased to see me, and so was Rosa Dartle. I was agreeably surprised to find that Littimer was not there, and that we were attended by a modest little parlour-maid, with blue ribbons in her cap.

Mrs. Steerforth was particularly happy in her son's society, and Steerforth was, on this occasion, particularly attentive and respectful to her.

This puzzled Miss. Dartle and she thought he had grow lukewarm towards her.

ᗅᗅᗅ

30

A Loss

In a letter Peggotty had informed me that her husband was in a hopeless state. So, I got down to Yarmouth in the evening, and went to the inn. It was ten o'clock. I came to Omer and Joram's, and met Omer. I expressed to him my sorrow for Mr. Barkis.

'You must always recollect of Em'ly,' said Mr. Omer, shaking his head gently, 'that she's a most extraordinary affectionate little thing.'

I asked Mr. Omer, whether he knew anything of Martha.

'Ah!' he rejoined, But then....his daughter Minnie and her husband came in.

Their report was, that Mr. Barkis was 'as bad as bad could be'; that he was quite unconscious.

Learning that Mr. Peggotty was there, I determined to go to the house at once.

'He's a going out with the tide,' said Mr Peggotty.

I shook hands with Mr. Peggotty. Little Emily and Ham were also there. Barkis was quite mute and senseless.

'He's a going out with the tide,' said Mr. Peggotty.

'Look! Here's Master Davy!' said Peggotty. For he now opened his eyes.

He tried to stretch out his arm, and said to me, distinctly, with a pleasant smile: 'Barkis is willin'! And, it being low water, he went out with the tide.

31

A Greater Loss

I tried to keep company with Peggotty till Barkis's remains were taken to Blunderstone.

I had a supreme satisfaction, in taking charge of Mr. Barkis's will, and expounding its contents. We were all to meet in the old boathouse that night. Ham would bring Emily at the usual hour. However, I was shocked to learn when Ham told me that Em'ly had run away.

Mr. Peggotty was in a miserable condition. In the midst of the silence of death, I read Em'ly' letter:

"Try to think as If I died when I was little. I'll pray for all. My parting love to uncle."

'Who's the man, Ham?' asked Mr. Peggotty.

'There's been a servant about here.'

'For the Lord's love,' said Mr. Peggotty, 'Don't tell me his name's Steerforth!' ❏❏❏

32

The Beginning of a Long Journey

The news of what had happened soon spread through the town. Ham said, 'If ever I encountered Steerforth, I will kill him."

'My dooty here, sir,' said Mr. Peggotty, 'is done. 'I'm a going to seek her.'

He purposed first seeing Mrs. Steerforth. I felt bound to assist him in this, and also to mediate between them.

Mr. Peggotty tried to convince Mrs. Steerforth that her son should now be married to his niece so that the occasion for disgrace could be arrested.

Then she said, 'Such a marriage would irretrievably blight my son's career, and ruin his prospects.'

There was a long discussion between Mr. Peggotty and Mrs Steerforth which proved futile.

33
Blissful

Taking the management of Peggotty's affairs into my own hands, I got everything into an orderly train.

She admired my horse and patted him.

Mr. Spenlow being a little drowsy after the champagne, and being fast asleep in a corner of the carriage, I rode by the side and talked to Dora, his daughter, with whom I had fallen in love.

She admired my horse and patted him.

Miss Mills called me to the other side of the carriage and said, 'Dora is coming to stay with me. She is coming home with me the day after tomorrow. If you would like to call, I am sure papa would be happy to see you.'

Norwood was many miles too near, and we reached it many hours too soon; but Mr. Spenlow came to himself a little short of it, and said, 'You must come in, Copperfield, and rest!' and I consenting, we had sandwiches and wine-and-water.

In the light room, Dora blushing looked so lovely, that I could not tear myself away, but sat there staring, in a dream, until the snoring of Mr. Spenlow inspired me with sufficient consciousness to take my leave.

So we parted; I riding all the way to London with the farewell touch of Dora's hand still light on mine.

34
My Aunt Astonishes Me

I wrote to Agnes as soon as Dora and I were engaged. I tried to make her comprehend what a darling Dora was.

While I had been away from home lately, Traddles had called twice or thrice. Talking about his fiancee, Sophy, Traddles told me, "She is much an extraordinary dear girl."

What was my amazement to find, of all people upon earth, my aunt with Mr. Dick sitting on a quantity of luggage, with her two birds before her, and her cat on her knee.

After exchange of formal salutations and tea, my aunt said to me, 'It's all I have. Because I'm ruined, my dear!'

'I am ruined, my dear Trot! All I have in the world is in this room, except the cottage; and that I have left Janet to let.'

❏❏❏

35
Depression

As I reached office, I told Spenlow about my aunt, say, 'She has met with some large losses. In fact, she has very little left, indeed.'

After talking to both Mr. Spenlow and Mr. Jorkins, I felt that the recovery of my aunt's thousand pounds was out of the question. In a state of despondency, I left the office, and went homeward.

Then Agnes came in a hackney-chariot.

She was going to my aunt who had written her a short letter mentioning her adversity and her leaving Dover room.

She was not alone, she said. Her papa was with her—and Uriah Heep.

'And now they are partners,' said I.

'Yes,' said Agnes. 'They have some business here; Actually, I do not like to let papa go away alone, with him.'

I told Spenlow about my aunt's large losses.

'There is such a change at home,' said she, They live with us now. Mr. Heep and his mother. He sleeps in your old room,' said Agnes.

'I keep my own little room,' said Agnes.

'The chief evil of their presence in the house,' said Agnes, 'is that I cannot be as near papa as I could wish—Uriah Heep being so much between us.'

We found my aunt alone. She explained in detail how she had fallen in adversity.

There was a long discussion among the aunt, Agnes and me as to what should be done now for the immediate future and the future on long term.

Agnes said, 'Doctor Strong has acted on his intention of retiring, and has come to live in London; and he asked papa, I know, if he could recommend him one.

Don't you think he would rather have his favourite old pupil near him, than anybody else?'

Acting on the advice of Agnes, I sat down and wrote a letter to the Doctor, stating my object, and appointing to call on him next day at ten in the forenoon.

As Wickfield and Uriah Heep came, my aunt said to Wickfield, 'I have been telling your daughter how well I have been disposing of my money for myself.'

However, Wickfield had full faith in Uriah Heep and he said, 'Uriah Heep is a great relief to me. It's a load off my mind, Trotwood, to have such a partner.'

36
Enthusiasm

The next day I started for Highgate. My first care was to find the Doctor's house.

He took me by both hands. I told him about my proposal.

'I shall be twenty times happier, sir,' said I, 'if my employment is to be on the Dictionary.'

The Doctor exclaimed, 'My dear young friend, you have hit it. It IS the Dictionary!'

Our plans were arranged to our mutual satisfaction. I wanted to know about reporting the debates in Parliament. But I learnt from Traddles after his inquries that it required a perfect and entire command.

Then Traddles, suddenly, brought a letter out of his pocket. It was from Mr. Micawber to me.

After a long introduction Mr. Micawber placed his I.O.U. in the hands of Traddles, and said he wished him well in every relation of life.

37

A Little Cold Water

My engagement with Dora, having been accomplished, I went to see her. She came to the drawing-room door to meet me; and Jip came scrambling out, and we all three went in, as happy and loving as could be. She seemed annoyed when I used the clause if she could love a beggar for myself.

I looked so serious, that Dora left off shaking her curls, and began to cry. I fell upon my knees before the sofa, caressing her, and imploring her not to rend my heart.

At last, after an agony of supplication and protestation, her soft, pretty cheek was lying against mine.

Well! I loved her, and I went on loving her, most absorbingly, entirely, and completely, but going on, too, working pretty hard.

38

A Dissolution of Partnership

I did not allow my resolution, with respect to the Parliamentary Debates, to cool.

When I had groped my way, blindly, through initial difficulties, and had mastered the alphabet, there then appeared a procession of new horrors, called arbitrary characters.

To make matter easy for me Traddles would, behave as one of the renowned politicians and deliver the most withering denunciations of the profligacy and corruption of my aunt and Mr. Dick; while I used to sit, at a little distance, with my notebook on my knee, fagging after him with all my might and main.

We pursued these debates till midnight, and the result of so much good practice was, that by and by I began to keep pace with Traddles pretty well.

Traddles would behave as one of the renowned politicians.

One day, when I went to the Commons as usual, I found Mr. Spenlow looking extremely grave. Miss Murdstone was there and on Spenlow's asking, she produced my letters to Dora, teeming with expressions of devoted affection. When I told him that I loved his daughter, he said, 'Pooh! nonsense!'

'Let there be an end of the nonsense. Take away those letters, and throw them in the fire.'

'Meanwhile, confer with Miss Trotwood, or with any person with any knowledge of life,' said Mr. Spenlow, 'Take a week, Mr. Copperfield.'

I submitted; and, with a countenance as expressive as I was able to make it, came out of the room.

It was Saturday morning, and I went straight to the Commons.

I was surprised, when I came within sight of our office-door, to see the ticket-porters standing outside talking together.

It was shocking to know that Mr. Spenlow was dead. Spenlow's private papers, whatever available were sealed by Mr. Jorkins.

One important thing missing was that perhaps there was no will.

⌐⌐⌐

39
Wickfield and Heep

A rrived at Mr. Wickfield's house, I found Mr. Micawber plying his pen with great assiduity. He told me that he had become the tenant of Uriah Heep's old house.

As Uriah Heep was following me when I was going to meet Agnes, I asked him. 'Do you suppose, that I regard Miss Wickfield otherwise than as a very dear sister?'

Then said I, 'I believe Agnes Wickfield to be far above you.'

I had observed yesterday, that he tried to entice Mr. Wickfield to drink. Mr. Wickfield was mad for the moment; tearing out his hair, beating his head after an altercation with Heep. Then Mr. Wickfield went out with Agnes.

'Heaven bless you!' she said, giving me her hand, and there is God to trust in!'.

'Can I do nothing?'

40

The Wanderer

Returning from Mr. Wickfield's house, I saw Mr. Peggotty! His hair was long and ragged, and his face was burnt dark and he had the appearance of having toiled and wandered through all varieties of weather; but he looked strong.

From some pocket in his breast, he took out, a small paper bundle containing some packets. The first one contained a fifty pound Bank note.

'This come to Missis Gummidge,' he said.

Some money was enclosed in another letter also. Five pounds.

He rose, and I rose too.

I went with him over Westminster Bridge, and parted from him on the Surrey shore, as he resumed his solitary journey through the snow.

41
Dora's Aunts

I wrote a letter to Dora's aunts. I wanted to seek permission to visit their place and meet Dora.

At last, an answer came from the two old ladies. The Misses Spenlow replied that if Mr. Copperfield would do them the favour to call, upon a certain day (accompanied, by a confidential friend), they would be happy to hold some conversation on the subject.

To this favour, I immediately replied, that I would have the honour of waiting on the Misses Spenlow, at the time appointed.

'Mr. Copperfield!' said the sister with the letter, 'My sister Lavinia,' said she 'being conversant with matters of this nature, will state what we consider most calculated to promote the happiness of both parties.'

I discovered afterwards that Miss Lavinia was an authority in affairs of the heart.

Then said Miss Lavinia, 'We have no reason to doubt, Mr. Copperfield, that you are a young gentleman possessed of good qualities and honourable character; or that you have an affection—for our niece.'

I replied, that nobody had ever loved anybody else as I loved Dora. Traddles came to my assistance with a confirmatory murmur.

Then Miss Lavinia, resumed : 'You ask permission of my sister Clarissa and myself, Mr. Copperfield, to visit here, as the accepted suitor of our niece.'

Miss Lavinia proceeded: 'Mr. Copperfield, after considering this letter we have shown it to our niece, and discussed it with her. We have no doubt that you think you like her very much.' Thereafter Traddles and Miss Lavinia had a long discussion when Traddles told her about his own engagement with Sophy.

'Then,' pursued Miss Lavinia,—'but, we must guard ourselves from recognizing any positive engagement between Mr. Copperfield and our

Thereafter Traddles and Miss Lavinia had a long discussion.

niece, until we have had an opportunity of observing them.'

Miss Lavinia then mentioned some practical condition, 'We must require from Mr. Copperfield a distinct assurance, on his word of honour, that no communication of any kind shall take place between him and our niece without our knowledge. That no project whatever shall be entertained with regard to our niece, without being first submitted to us—'

I bound myself by the required promise, in a most impassioned manner and called upon Traddles to witness it.

'In the course of the week,' said Miss Clarissa, 'we shall be happy to see Mr. Copperfield to tea. Our hour is half-past six.'

'Twice in the week,' said Miss Clarissa, 'but, as a rule, not oftener.'

'Miss Trotwood,' said Miss Clarissa, 'mentioned in Mr. Copperfield's letter, will perhaps call upon us.

I intimated that my aunt would be proud and delighted to make their acquaintance.

Miss Lavinia then arose, and begging Mr. Traddles to excuse us for a minute, requested me to follow her. I obeyed, all in a tremble, and was conducted into another room. There I found my blessed darling shedding her tears behind the door. Oh! How beautiful she was in her black frock. 'My dearest Dora! Now, indeed, my own for ever!'

⊐⊐⊐

42
Mischief

Agnes came on a visit of a fortnight to the Doctor's. Mr. Wickfield was the Doctor's old friend, and the Doctor wished to talk with him, and do him good.

She and her father came together. I was not much surprised to hear from her that she had engaged to find a lodging in the neighbourhood for Mrs. Heep, whose rheumatic complaint required change of air. Neither was I surprised when, Uriah, like a dutiful son, brought his worthy mother to take possession.

Dora was afraid of Agnes. She had told me that she knew Agnes was 'too clever'. But when she saw her looking at once so cheerful and so earnest, and so thoughtful, and so good, she gave a faint little cry of pleased surprise, and just put her affectionate arms round Agnes's neck, and laid her innocent cheek against her face.

I never was so happy. I never was so pleased as when I saw those two sit down together, side by side.

There was a hurried but affectionate parting between Agnes and Dora.

As we reached the Highgate, It was growing late. There was a light in the window of Mrs. Strong's chamber, and Agnes, pointing to it, bade me good night.

Then, I saw a light in the Doctor's study.

I gently opened the door, and looked in.

The first person whom I saw, to my surprise, was Uriah.

The Doctor sat in his study chair, covering his face with his hands. Mr. Wickfield, sorely troubled and distressed, was leaning forward, irresolutely touching the Doctor's arm.

'I mentioned to Doctor Strong,' Uriah said, 'that anyone may see that Mr. Maldon, and Annie, are too sweet on one another.

'Mr. Maldon made excuses to come back, for nothing else; and that he's always here, for nothing else.'

In the morning, the Doctor gave out that he was not quite well; and remained alone.

Mrs. Strong she seemed to wonder at the gentle compassion with which the Doctor spoke to her, and at his wish that she should have her mother with her, to relieve the dull monotony of her life.

Afterwards, I sometimes observed her rise, with her eyes full of tears, and go out of the room. Gradually, an unhappy shadow fell upon her beauty, and deepened every day.

The Doctor became older in appearance, but the sweetness of his temper, and his benevolent solicitude for Annie, were increased.

Meanwhile, I received a letter from Mrs. Micawber from which I learnt that 'Mr. Micawber is entirely changed. He is reserved. He is secret. His life is a mystery to the partner of his joys and sorrows—that is his wife.

He is estranged from our eldest son and daughter, he has no pride in his twins, The pecuniary means of meeting our expenses, kept down to the utmost farthing, are obtained from him with great difficulty.

I advised her that she should try to reclaim Mr. Micawber by patience and kindness; but the letter set me thinking about him very much.

43

Another Retrospect

I have come legally to man's estate. I have attained the dignity of twenty-one. Let me think what I have achieved.

I have tamed that savage stenographic mystery. I make a respectable income by it. I am in high repute for my accomplishment in all pertaining to the art, and am joined with eleven others in reporting the debates in Parliament for a Morning Newspaper.

I have come out in another way. I have taken with fear and trembling to authorship. I wrote a little something, in secret, and sent it to a magazine, and it was published in the magazine.

Since then, I have taken heart to write a good many trifling pieces. Now, I am regularly paid for them. Altogether, I am well off.

We have removed, from Buckingham Street, to a pleasant little cottage very near the one I looked at, when my enthusiasm first came on.

Yes! I am going to be married to Dora! Miss Lavinia and Miss Clarissa have given their consent.

The realization of my boyish day-dreams is at hand. I am going to take out the licence.

Sophy arrives at the house of Dora's aunts, in due course. She has the most agreeable of faces,—not absolutely beautiful, but extraordinarily pleasant.

I have brought Agnes from the Canterbury coach, and her cheerful and beautiful face is among us for the second time. Agnes has a great liking for Traddles.

We drive away together, and I awake from the dream. I believe it at last. It is my dear, dear, little wife beside me, whom I love so well!

❒❒❒

44
Our Housekeeping

The honeymoon being over, and the bride-smaids gone home, I found myself sitting down in my own small house with Dora.

We had a servant, of course. We had such an awful time of it with Mary Anne.

She preyed upon our minds dreadfully. She was the cause of our first little quarrel.

I felt I had wounded Dora's soft little heart, and she was not to be comforted. She was pathetic in her bewailing.

The next domestic trial we went through, was the Ordeal of Servants. Mary Anne's cousin deserted into our coal-hole, and was brought out, to our great amazement, by a piquet of his companions in arms, who took him away handcuffed in a procession that covered our front-garden with ignominy. This nerved me to get rid of Mary Anne, who went

Dora was going to be a wonderful housekeeper.

so mildly, on receipt of wages, that I was surprised, until I found out about the tea-spoons, and also about the little sums she had borrowed in my name of the tradespeople without authority.

Everybody we had anything to do with seemed to cheat us. Our appearance in a shop was a signal for the damaged goods to be brought out immediately. If we bought a lobster, it was full of water. All our meat turned out to be tough, and there was hardly any crust to our loaves.

I had reason to believe that in accomplishing these failures we incurred a far greater expense than if we had achieved a series of triumphs. One of our first feats in the housekeeping way was a little dinner to Traddles in which Dora showed her skill.

It was a great thing for me when Dora told me, that she was going to be a wonderful housekeeper. Accordingly, she polished the tablets, pointed the pencil, bought an immense account-book, carefully stitched up with a needle and thread all the leaves of the Cookery Book which Jip had torn, and made quite a desperate little attempt 'to be good', as she called it. But the figures had the old obstinate propensity—they WOULD NOT add up.

45

Mr. Dick Fulfils
My Aunt's Predictions

One day Mr. Dick told me that there was an unhappy separation between doctor and his wife for an unknown reason. 'But 'I'll bring them together, boy,' he said.

Just then we heard the coach brought my aunt and Dora home.

One fair evening, my aunt and I strolled up to the Doctor's cottage. It was twilight.

We saw the Doctor, sitting at his table. Then we saw Mrs. Strong glide in, pale and trembling. Mr. Dick supported her on his arm. As the Doctor moved his head, his wife dropped down on one knee at his feet.

She said imploringly, 'Oh, my husband and father, break this long silence. Let us both know what it is that has come between us!'

'Annie!' said the Doctor, tenderly taking her in his hands. 'My dear! If any unavoidable change has come, in the sequence of time, upon our married life, you are not to blame. The fault is mine, and only mine.'

'Mrs. Strong,' I said, 'there is something within my knowledge, which I have been earnestly entreated by Doctor Strong to conceal.' On her insistence I gave an explanation.

When I had finished, Annie took the Doctor's hand and pressed it to her breast, and kissed it. Mr. Dick softly raised her.

Then Annie spoke with such sincerity that all knew that is was plain truth confirming her faultlessness.

It was all conciliation when she cried out, 'Oh, hold me to your heart, my husband! Never cast me out! Do not think or speak of disparity between us, for there is none, except in all my many imperfections,' she exclamied.

In the silence that ensued, my aunt walked gravely up to Mr. Dick.

'You are a very remarkable man, Dick!' said my aunt.'

ᄀᄀᄀ

46
Intelligence

One evening, as I was returning from a solitary walk, I came past Mrs. Steerforth's house. A female voice called me. I was presented to Miss Rosa Dartle who asked Littimer to tell me the story of Em'ly.

Littimer said, 'Mr. James and myself have been abroad with the young woman, ever since she left Yarmouth under Mr. James's protection. We have been in a variety of places, and even in France, Switzerland, Italy.

After some time the woman and James both got weary of each other. Still matters were patched up here, and made good there, over and over again; and lasted, for a long time. At last, when there had been, a good many words and reproaches, Mr. James he set off one morning, making an excuse, and never came back.

Miss Rosa asked Littimer to tell me the story of Em'ly.

The young woman's violence after I broke the fact of his departure, was beyond all expectations. She was quite mad, and had to be held by force.

Still, she escaped and never has been seen or heard of since.

'She is dead, perhaps,' said Miss Dartle.

I felt it right that it should be communicated to Mr. Peggotty. On the following evening I went into London in quest of him.

He listened in profound silence to all I had to tell. Then we began to contemplate where she was likely to go. I said that she was most likely to come to Martha because she had been charitable to her with Ham's help.

'Do you know that she is in London?' I asked.

'I have seen her in the streets,' he answered, with a shiver.

'It is dark. Being together, shall we go out now, and try to find her tonight?' I said. He assented, and prepared to accompany me.

We were not far from Blackfriars Bridge, when he turned his head and pointed to a solitary female figure flitting along the opposite side of the street. I knew it, was Martha.

We crossed the road, and were pressing on towards her. Then me decided to speak to her but she turned into a dull, dark street, where the noise and crowd were lost; and I said, 'We may speak to her now'; and, mending our pace, we went after her.   ▭▭▭

47
Martha

We had turned back to follow Martha. She soon went slowly along by the brink of the river.

When I said 'Martha!' she uttered a terrified scream.

'I should have been in the river long ago,' she said, 'if any wrong to her had been upon my mind.'

'The cause of her flight is too well understood,' I said. 'You are innocent of any part in it, we thoroughly believe,—we know.'

'She was always good to me! She never spoke an unpleasant word to me. The people would remember she once kept company with me, and would say I had corrupted her!'

Suddenly she turned to my companion. 'Stamp upon me, kill me!'

'Martha,' said Mr. Peggotty, 'God forbid as I should judge you.'

He spoke so politely to her that his influence upon her was complete. Her passionate sorrow was quite hushed and mute.

'According to our reckoning,' he proceeded, 'She is likely, one day, to make her own poor solitary course to London. Help us all you can to find her, and may Heaven reward you!'

'To speak to her, if I should ever find her; and then, without her knowledge, come to you, and bring you to her?' she asked hurriedly.

We both replied together, 'Yes!'

She asked, when all was told, where we were to be communicated with, if occasion should arise. Under a dull lamp in the road, I wrote our two addresses on a leaf of my pocket-book, which I tore out and gave to her, and which she put in her poor bosom. I asked her where she lived herself. But she refused to tell. We tried to give her some money but she refused to accept it. It was midnight when I arrived at home.

Thinking that my aunt might have relapsed into one of her old alarms, I went to speak to her. It was with very great surprise that I saw a man standing in her little garden.

I recognized the man whom I had once supposed to be a delusion of Mr. Dick's, and had once encountered with my aunt in the streets of the city. She was giving him some money but he was demanding more. But in view of her heavy losses, she could give no more.

I met him at the gate, and went in as he came out. I asked her who the man was.

Then she came out, and said, 'Trot, it's my husband.' 'Your husband, aunt? I thought he had been dead!'

'Dead to me,' returned my aunt, 'but living.'

She further said that once she loved him intensely but he broke her heart. He treated her cruelly. 'I believe, he became an adventurer, a gambler, and a cheat,' said my aunt.

'He is nothing to me now. But, sooner than have him punished for his offences I give him more money than I can afford, at intervals when he reappears, to go away.'

'There, my dear!' she said. 'We won't mention the subject to one another any more; neither, of course, will you mention it to anybody else.'

48
Domestic

As for my domestic life, I laboured hard at my book, and it came out and was very

I began to carry her downstairs every morning and upstairs every night.

successful. We engaged a page but he had burgalrious intentions and was tried and ordered to be transported.

I resolved to form Dora's mind by reading, but to no purpose. I bought a pretty pair of ear-rings for her, and she was delighted with the little presents, and kissed me joyfully; but there was a shadow between us, however slight, and I had made up my mind that it should not be there. 'The truth is, Dora, my life,' I said; 'I have been trying to be wise.'

'And to make me wise too,' said Dora, timidly. 'Haven't you, Doady?'

She put her arms round my neck, and laughed, and called herself by her favourite name of a goose.

Later, she fell ill and couldn't walk. Then I began to carry her downstairs every morning, and upstairs every night. She would clasp me round the neck and laugh. But a dead blank feeling came upon me, as if I were approaching to some frozen region yet unseen, that numbed my life.

ꓱꓱꓱ

49

I am Involved in Mystery

One morning I received a letter from Micawber. In it he wrote:

'Among other havens of domestic tranquillity and peace of mind, my feet will naturally tend towards the King's Bench Prison. In stating that I shall be (D.V.) on the outside of the south wall of that place of incarceration on civil process, the day after tomorrow, at seven in the evening,'

I approached Traddles. He had received a letter from Mrs. Micawber that said nothing of it.

However, she wrote Mr. Micawber had sold himself to the D. Mystery and secrecy have long been his pricipal characteristic.

We found Mr. Micawber at the place before the time. He felt excited when I said to him, 'How is our friend Heep, Mr. Micawber?'

We took him to my aunt's house. My aunt welcomed Mr. Micawber with gracious cordiality.

Mr. Dick who was there tried to exhort Mr. Micawber who seemed in low spirits.

'Mr. Micawber,' said I, 'what is the matter? Pray speak out. You are among friends.'

'Villainy is the matter; baseness is the matter; deception, fraud, conspiracy, are the matter; and the name of the whole atrocious mass is—HEEP!'

'I'll put my hand in no man's hand,' he continued, 'until I have—blown to fragments—the—a—detestable—serpent—HEEP!'

I really had some fear of Mr. Micawber's dying on the spot. I would have gone to his assistance, but he waved me off, and wouldn't hear a word.

Then Mr. Micawber rushed out of the house; and sent a note saying.

'An explosion of a smouldering volcano long suppressed, was the result of an internal contest more easily conceived than descri-bed.....so on.

'WILKINS MICAWBER.'

50

Mr. Peggotty's Dream Comes True

I was walking alone in the garden. I heard Martha calling me. She said that she had been to Mr. Peggotty and he was not at home. "I wrote down where he was to come, and left it on his table with my own hand."

She took me anywhere near the Golden Square! We proceeded to the top-storey. I was amazed to see there Miss Rosa Dartle, who had just entered. She started hurling taunts and reproaches on somebody. It was Emly. She even tried to run away but in vain and Rosa even tried to hit her.

'Oh, for Heaven's sake, spare me!' exclaimed Emily. Would he (Steerforth) never, never come? How long was I to bear this? 'What, shall I do!'

'Marry that good man, and be happy in his condescension. If this will not do, die!,' said Rosa.

'I thank my Heav'nly Father as my dream's come true!'

I heard a distant foot upon the stairs. I saw him supporting her insensible figure in his arms. I thank my Heav'nly Father as my dream's come true!' he said.

He took her up in his arms; and carried her, motionless and unconscious, down the stairs.

51

The Beginning of
a Longer Journey

Mr. Peggotty, told my aunt the story of Em'ly. 'When my Em'ly took flight in the night, she ran along the sea beach.

The day broke, and she was lying upon the shore and a woman was a-speaking to her.

'She—took her home.' Em'ly was took bad with fever. The language of that country went out of her head, and she was forced to make signs.

The husband was come home, then; and the two together put her aboard a small trader bound to Leghorn, and from that to France. Then she come to London. She found a friend; a decent woman—Martha, trew to her promise, saved her.'

Then she went in search of me; then in search of you, Mas'r Davy. She didn't tell Em'ly what she come out fur, lest her 'art should fail, and she should think of hiding of herself.'

❏❏❏

52

I Assist at an Explosion

My aunt, Mr. Dick, Traddles, and I, went down to Canterbury that night, and reached the hotel where Mr. Micawber had requested us to await him.

At exact half past nine, he appeared.

He gave Mr. Dick a new name 'Mr. Dixon' which pleased him greatly.

'Mr. Copperfield,' said Mr. Micawber, 'I would beg to be allowed a start of five minutes; inquiring for Miss Wickfield, at the office of Wickfield and Heep, whose Stipendiary I am.'

As we all went out together to the old house, we found Mr. Micawber at his desk. Our visit astonished Uriah Heep. He tried to bully Mr. Micawber. This led to a heated exchange of words between the two.

Our visit atonished Uriah Heep.

'Miss Wickfield, if you have any love for your father, you had better not join that gang. I'll ruin him, if you do,' said Heep.

'Think twice, you, Micawber, if you don't want to be crushed,' he said, and called his mother.

'I am the agent and friend of Mr. Wickfield, sir,' said Traddles. 'And I have a power of attorney from him in my pocket, to act for him in all matters.'

Mr. Micawber, produced from his pocket a foolscap document and began to read.

Mr. Micawber explained in his letter the circumstances under which he became a clerk to Uriah Heep and how the latter has cheated him. Uriah went to the iron safe in the room. It was empty. 'Where are the books?' he cried, 'Some thief has stolen the books!'

'Don't be uneasy,' said Traddles. 'They have come into my possession. I will take care of them, under the authority I mentioned.'

What was my astonishment when I beheld my aunt, make a dart at Uriah Heep, and seize him by the collar with both hands!

'You know what I want?' said my aunt. 'My property!' Then Uriah said to me : 'What do you want done?'

'What must be done,' said Traddles, 'is this. First, the deed of relinquishment, that we have heard of, must be given over to me now—here.'

'Then,' continued Traddles, 'you must prepare to disgorge all that your rapacity has become possessed of, and to make restoration to the last farthing. All the partnership books and papers must remain in our possession; all your books and papers; all money accounts and securities, of both kinds. In short, everything here.'

'Copperfield, will you go round to the Guildhall, and bring a couple of officers?' said Traddles.

Here, Mrs. Heep broke out, crying on her knees to Agnes to interfere in their behalf, exclaiming that he was very humble.

'Stop!' he growled to me; 'Mother, hold your noise. Well! Let 'em have that deed. Go and fetch it!' Mr. Dick accompanied Mrs. Heep and she not only returned with the deed, but with the box in which it was, where we found a banker's book and some other papers that were afterwards serviceable. My aunt mused a little while, and then said:

'Mr. Micawber, I wonder you have never turned your thoughts to emigration.Urged Mr. Micawber, gloomily, 'If it could be.'

'Could be? Can be and shall be,' returned my aunt. Here are some people David knows, going out to Australia shortly. If you decide to go, why shouldn't you go in the same ship? You may help each other.'   ▢▢▢

53

Another Retrospect

I am again with Dora the Little Blossom, in our cottage. I do not know how long she has been ill. I long to see my child-wife running in the sunlight with her old friend Jip. He is, as it were suddenly, grown very old.

Dora lies smiling on us, and is beautiful, and utters no hasty or complaining word. It is morning; and Dora has been made so trim by my aunt's hands. In the evening; I sit beside her. She lies here all the day.

It is night; and I am with her still. Agnes has arrived; has been among us for a whole day and an evening. We have not talked much.

Do I know, now, that my child-wife will soon leave me? They have told me so. It is over. Darkness comes before my eyes; and, for a time, all things are blotted out of my remembrance.

Agnes and I only pray to Heaven. ꓘꓘꓘ

54

Mr. Micawber's Transactions

My aunt, Agnes, and I proceeded to Mr. Micawber's house. Mr. Micawber thanked my aunt for the pecuniary assistance.

Mr. Micawber began to talk about various minutae of the memorandum. My aunt observed, that in a case where both parties were willing to agree to anything, she took it for granted there would be no difficulty in settling this point. Mr. Micawber was of her opinion.

At nine, my aunt and I we went out in a little chariot, and drove to London. We drove to one of the large hospitals. Standing hard by the building was a plain hearse.

My aunt's husband had died in that hospital. 'Six-and-thirty years ago, this day.

So we rode back to her little cottage at Highgate, where we found note from Mr. Micawber. In it he mentioned:

Standing hard by the building was a plain hearse.

'Mr. Thomas Traddles has paid the debt and costs, in the noble name of Miss Trotwood; and that myself and family are at the height of earthly bliss.'

55

Tempest

I wrote to Em'ly about what had passed between Ham and me when I was last at Yarmouth.

Then Mr. Peggotty gave me Em'ly's reply. The letter ended thus : Now, my dear, my friend, good-bye for ever in this world. In another world, if I am forgiven, I may wake a child and come to you. All thanks and blessings. Farewell, evermore.'

I went to Yarmouth to put this letter of her writing in Ham's hand and tell her, in the moment of parting, that he has got it. It was an evening of murky confusion of flying clouds. When the day broke, it blew harder and harder.

Coming near the beach, I found bewailing men and women. But I did not find Ham among the people. Then I made my way to his house but he was not there also.

As the news spread that two men were gone, Two men were gone, the agony on the shore increased. Men and women ran wildly up and down along the beach, crying for help. I found myself one of these.

Then I noticed Ham come breaking through them to the front. I held him back with both arms; and implored the men with whom I had been speaking, not to listen to him, not to do murder, not to let him stir from off that sand!

I perceived, that he was bent on going, with help or without, I saw hurry on the beach. And now he made for the wreck.

After a long struggle but then a high, green, vast hill-side of water, emerged moving on shoreward, from beyond the ship, and as he seemed to leap up into the ship it was gone!

Consternation was in every face. They drew him to my very feet—insensible—dead. He had been beaten to death by the great wave, and his generous heart was stilled for ever.

Then I learnt about another body that came ashore. It was Steerforth.

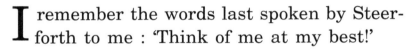

56

The New Wound, and the Old

I remember the words last spoken by Steerforth to me : 'Think of me at my best!'

They brought a hand-bier, and laid him on it.

I took upon myself the hard duty of preparing his mother to receive it. I chose the night for the journey to London.

It was with great difficulty that I broke the news. Immediately on hearing it, Mrs. Steerforth turned into a statue who would not see or hear.

As for Miss Rosa Dartle, she burst out into a violent hysteric. She blamed me and Mrs Steerforth. She expressed her emotion, explaining how she loved Steerforth but her love was smothered in its infancy. I tried to calm her down but she would not listen to me.

As for Mrs. Steerforth, doctors were in attendance, when I left the place.   ❐❐❐

57

The Emigrants

Before starting for the new country, Mr. Micawber drew a note-of-hand with great neatness, which he handed over to Traddles on the spot, a discharge of his debt in full, with many acknowledgements.

Mr. Peggotty was waiting for us on the deck. He told me that Mr. Micawber had just now been arrested again (and for the last time) at the suit of Heep, and that, in compliance with a request I had made to him, he had paid the money, which I repaid him.

The time was come, I embraced him. As the sails rose to the wind, and the ship began to move, there broke from all the boats three resounding cheers.

Then I saw her, at her uncle's side, Aye, Emily, beautiful and drooping, cling to him with the utmost trust of thy bruised heart. ❑❑❑

58
Absence

I went away from England; not knowing, even then, how great the shock was, that I had to bear. I left all who were dear to me, and went away.

For many months I travelled and travelled.

I was in Switzerland. I had come out of Italy, over one of the great passes of the Alps, and had since wandered with a guide among the by-ways of the mountains.

I came into the valley, as the evening sun was shining on the remote heights of snow, Nature spoke to me; and soothed me to lay down my weary head upon the grass, and weep as I had not wept yet, since Dora died!

I had found a packet of letters awaiting me but a few minutes before. It was from Agnes.

She was happy and useful, was prospering as she had hoped.

She gave me no advice; she urged no duty on me; she only told me, in her own fervent manner, what her trust in me was.

I wrote to her I told her that I had been in sore need of her help; that without her I was not, and I never had been, what she thought me; but that she inspired me to be that, and I would try.

I decided to settle myself for the present in Switzerland, to resume my pen; to work.

I resorted humbly whither Agnes had commended me; that is to Nature.

I wrote a Story, and sent it to Traddles, and he arranged for its publication very advantageously for me; and the tidings of my growing reputation began to reach me from travellers whom I encountered by chance.

Meanwhile working patiently, I had improved my health.

Three years. Long in the aggregate, though short as they went by. And home was very dear to me, and Agnes too—but she was not mine—she was never to be mine. She might have been, but that was past!

⊐⊐⊐

59
Return

I landed in London on a wintry autumn evening. It was dark and raining.

My aunt had long been re-established at Dover, and Traddles had begun to get into some little practice at the Bar. He had chambers in Gray's Inn, now.

I alighted at the door of the Gray's Inn Coffee-house. I went to see Traddles. I was glad to learn from him that he was married.

The dearest girl in the world came at that same instant, laughing and blushing.

'The girls,' said Traddles, 'Sophy's sisters, they are staying with us. They have come to have a peep at London.

And Sophy's an extraordinary manager! You'll be surprised how those girls are stowed away.'

□□□

60
Agnes

My aunt and I, when we were left alone, talked far into the night about emigrants Mr. Micawber's 'pecuniary liabilities', etc.

According to my aunt Mr. Wickfield was now a white-haired old man though a better man in all other respects—a reclaimed man.

I learnt from my aunt that 'Agnes had a score of suitors and she might have married twenty times, my dear, since you have been gone!' 'No doubt,' said I. But has she any lover who is worthy of her?'

'I suspect she has an attachment, Trot.'

'A prosperous one?' said I.

'Trot,' returned my aunt gravely, 'I can't say.' Then my aunt and I went to see Agnes. She was overjoyed to see us. I folded her to my heart, and, for a little while, we were both silent.

"I told her that she had to work hard at books.

I folded her to my heart and for a little while,
we were both silent.

'The labour is so pleasant,' she returned.'

'Nothing good is difficult to you,' said I. 'Here are the old books, Trotwood, and the old music.' 'And every little thing that has reminded me of my brother,' said Agnes, 'has been a welcome companion.'

It was for me to guard this sisterly affection with religious care. I walked through the streets. When I returned, Mr. Wickfield had come home from a garden.

There was tranquillity and peace belonging, of old there. When dinner was done, Mr. Wickfield taking no wine, and I desiring none, we went up-stairs; where Agnes sang and played, and worked. After tea we three sat together, talking of the bygone days.

He said, 'No one knows, not even you,' he returned, 'how much she has done, how much she has undergone, how hard she has striven. Dear Agnes!'

'Well! I have never told you, Trotwood, of her mother.' 'She married me in opposition to her father's wish, and he renounced her. She prayed him to forgive her, before my Agnes came into this world. He was a very hard man, and her mother had long been dead. He repulsed her. He broke her heart.'

'She had an affectionate and gentle heart,' he said; 'and it was broken. She loved me dearly, but was never happy, and she left me Agnes, two weeks old.'

Agnes rose up from her father's side, before long; and going softly to her piano, played some of the old airs.

She was against my going away again, and I agreed with her.

'What I am, you have made me, Agnes.'

She put her hand in mine, and told me she was proud of me.

For an instant, a distressful shadow crossed her face; but, even in the start it gave me, it was gone; and she was playing on, and looking at me with her own calm smile.

As I rode back in the lonely night, the wind going by me like a restless memory, I thought of this, and feared she was not happy. I was not happy; but, thus far, I had faithfully set the seal upon the Past, and thinking of her, pointing upward, thought of her as pointing to that sky above me, where, in the mystery to come, I might yet love her with a love unknown on earth, and tell her what that strife had been within me when I loved her here.

61

I Am Shown Two Interesting Penitents

For a time—I took up my abode in my aunt's house at Dover; I truly devoted myself to writing my book with my strongest earnestness, and bestowed upon it every energy of my soul. Occasionally, I went to London; to lose myself in the swarm of life there, or to consult Traddles on some business point.

One day Traddles showed me Sophy's handwriting which was legal and formal. I was glad to learn that Sophy was training heartily to be Traddles' copyclerk, whom he'd need after sometime.

Then I revealed to Traddles I had a letter from Mr. Creakle, who was not a school master but a Middlesex Magistrate. He had got this situation by having been nominated to this commission.

'And he writes to me here, said I that 'he will be glad to show me, in operation, the only true system of prison discipline; the only unchallengeable way of making sincere and lasting converts and penitents—which, you know, is by solitary confinement.' What do you say?' to my accepting the offer, and your going with me?'

'I don't object,' said Traddles.

'Then I'll write to say so. You remember this same Creakle turning his son out of doors, and the life he used to lead his wife and daughter?'

'Perfectly,' said Traddles.

'Yet, if you'll read his letter, you'll find he is the tenderest of men to prisoners convicted of the whole calendar of felonies,' said I.

On the appointed day—Traddles and I repaired to the prison where Mr. Creakle was all powerful. It was an immense and solid building, erected at a vast expense. I could not help thinking, as we approached the gate, what an uproar would have been made in the country, if any deluded man had proposed to spend one half the money it had cost, on the erection of an industrial school for the young, or a house of refuge for the deserving old.

In an office that might have been on the ground-floor of the Tower of Babel, it was so massivly constructed, we were presented to our old schoolmaster; who was one of a group, composed of two or three of the busier sort of magistrates, and some visitors they had brought. He received me, like a man who had formed my mind in bygone years, and had always loved me tenderly. On my introducing Traddles, Mr. Creakle expressed, in like manner, but in an inferior degree, that he had always been Traddles's guide, philosopher and friend.

After some conversation among these gentlemen, I might have supposed that there was nothing in the world to be legitimately taken into account but the supreme comfort of prisoners, at any expense. Thus we began our inspection. At dinner the prisoners were provided with plentiful repasts of choice quality.

As we were going through some of the magnificent passages, I inquired of Mr. Creakle and his friends what were supposed to be the main advantages of this all-governing and universally over-riding system? I found them to be the perfect isolation of prisoners—so that no one man in confinement there, knew anything about another; and the reduction of prisoners to a wholesome state of mind, leading to sincere contrition and repentance.

Then we visited a certain Number Twenty Seven

Then we visited a certain Number Twenty
Seven, who really appeared to be a Model
Prisoner. He constantly wrote beautiful letters
to his mother (whom he seemed to consider in
a very bad way). As we came to the door of his
cell; Mr. Creakle, looking through a little hole

in it, reported to us, in a state of the greatest admiration, that he was reading a Hymn Book.

Traddles and I then beheld, to our amazement, in this converted Number Twenty Seven, but Uriah Heep! I had been so much astonished already, that I only felt a kind of resigned wonder when Mr. Littimer walked forth, reading a good book! He was number 'Twenty Eight,'

I observed that several gentlemen were shading their eyes, each with one hand, as if they had just come into church. 'This does you credit, Twenty Eight,' returned the questioner. 'I should have expected it of you.'

From the behaviour of the two prisoners it appeared that they did not know each other.

Uriah expressed the desire to write one more letter to his mother, asking her to come here. He said, 'I wish mother had come here. It would be better for everybody.'

Then he added, 'There's a deal of sin outside. There's nothing but sin everywhere—except here.' He sneaked back into his cell, amidst a little chorus of approbation; and both Traddles and I experienced a great relief when he was locked in.
▢▢▢

62

A Light Shines on My Way

It was Christmas-time. During my talk with my aunt, she said to me, 'I think Agnes is going to be married.'

'God bless her!' said I, cheerfully.

I rode to Agnes. I found her alone.

I said to her, 'My dear Agnes, do you doubt my being true to you?'

'No!' she answered.

She said that she had always got my help and counsel whenever I needed it. So, she could not lose faith in me. I had so far loved her as my sister, though I could accept her as more than a sister. I tried to show her how I had hoped I had come into the better knowledge of myself and of her; If she did so love me (I said) that she could take me for her husband, she could do so, on no deserving of mine, except upon the truth of my love for her.

'I am so blest, Trotwood—my heart is so overcharged—but there is one thing I must say.'

'I have loved you all my life!'

O, we were happy, we were happy!

We stood together in the same old-fashioned window at night, when the moon was shining. It was nearly dinner-time next day when we appeared before my aunt.

Then, we were all happy together.

We were married within a fortnight. Traddles and Sophy, and Doctor and Mrs. Strong, were the only guests at our quiet wedding. We left them full of joy; and drove away together. Clasped in my embrace, I held the source of every worthy aspiration I had ever had; the centre of myself, the circle of my life, my own, my wife; my love of whom was founded on a rock!

'Dearest husband!' said Agnes. 'I have one thing more to tell you.'

'It was what Dora said to me before her death.'

'She told me that she left me something.

'That only I would occupy this vacant place.'

Both of us shed tears of happiness. ⊐⊐⊐

63

A Visitor

I had advanced in fame and fortune, my domestic joy was perfect. I had been married ten happy years. Agnes and I were sitting by the fire, in our house in London, one night in spring, and three of our children were playing in the room, when I was told that a stranger wished to see me.

It was Mr. Peggotty. An old man now, but in a ruddy, hearty, strong old age. When our first emotion was over, and he sat before the fire with the children on his knees, our conversation started.

'Are you going back those many thousand miles, so soon?' asked Agnes.

'Yes, ma'am,' he returned. 'I giv the promise to Em'ly, afore I come away.'

'And now tell us,' said I, 'everything relating to your fortunes.'

'Our fortuns, Mas'r Davy,' he rejoined. What with sheep-farming, and what with stock-farming, and what with one thing and what with t'other, we are as well to do, as well could be.'

'And Emily?' said Agnes and I, both together.

'Theer shining sundown—was that low, at first, that, if she had know'd then what Mas'r Davy kep from us so kind and thowtful, 'tis my opinion she'd have drooped away. But theer was some poor folks aboard as had illness among 'em, and she took care of them; and theer was the children in our company, and she took care of them; and so she got to be busy, and to be doing good, and that helped her.'

'Is she so altered?' I inquired.

'I doen't know. I see her ev'ry day, and A slight figure,' said Mr. Peggotty, 'kiender worn; soft, sorrowful, blue eyes; a delicate face; a pritty head, leaning a little down; a quiet voice and way—timid a'most. That's Em'ly!'

We silently observed him as he sat, still looking at the fire.

'Some thinks,' he said, 'as her affection was ill-bestowed; some, as her marrige was broken off my death. No one knows how 'tis. She might have married well, a mort of times, "but, uncle," she says to me, "that's gone for ever."

'Teaching children, tending the sick and helping others~that's what Em'ly is doing. As for Martha, she married a farm labourer in the second year."

There was a loud laughter when Mr. Peggotty told about Mrs. Gummidge. A ship's cook, proposed her. Instead of saying, 'Thank you or any other polite words to him, she emptied a bucket on his head.'

The most exciting news which was collected from a newspaper produced by Mr. Peggotty was that Mr. Micawber had become a magistrate in Australia. As Mr. Peggotty pointed to another part of the paper, my eyes rested on my own name, and I read thus:

'TO DAVID COPPERFIELD, ESQUIRE,

'THE EMINENT AUTHOR.

'My Dear Sir,..............

'WILKINS MICAWBER,

'Magistrate.'

I found, on glancing at the remaining contents of the newspaper, that Mr. Micawber was a diligent and esteemed correspondent of that journal. The Leading Article was also his. ⊐⊐⊐

64

A Last Retrospect

And now my written story ends. I look back, once more—for the last time.

I see myself, with Agnes at my side, journeying along the road of life. I see our children and our friends around us; and I hear the roar of many voices, not indifferent to me as I travel on.

Some faces are the most distinct to me in the fleeting crowd, while others are not.

My lamp burns low, and I have written far into the night; but the dear presence, without which I were nothing, bears me company.

O Agnes, O my soul, so may thy face be by me when I close my life indeed.

❑❑❑

GLOSSARY
(word-meanings)

1.	*Conveyed*	=	carried, took
2.	*Recollect*	=	remember
3.	*Originated*	=	started
4.	*Cordial*	=	sincere
5.	*Discontented*	=	dissatisfied
6.	*Disposition*	=	nature
7.	*Gloomy*	=	sad
8.	*Affectionate*	=	lovable
9.	*Petition*	=	application
10.	*Portable*	=	that can be carried
11.	*Delightful*	=	happy
12.	*Stretch out*	=	spread
13.	*Expound*	=	explain
14.	*Varieties*	=	kinds
15.	*Entire*	=	complete
16.	*Attained*	=	gained, got
17.	*Incarceration*	=	imprisonment
18.	*Tranquillity*	=	calmness
19.	*Indifferent*	=	careless
20.	*Esteemed*	=	respected

Short Questions

1. Describe Miss Trotwood's (or Miss Betsey's) visit to author's house.

2. Describe David's remembrance of Peggotty and Murdstone.

3. Describe David's visit to Yarmouth.

4. Describe David's home-study under Mr. Murdstone and his sister.

5. Describe David's visit to the Salem House during holidays.

6. Describe the death of David's mother.

7. Describe Micawber's arrest.

8. Describe David's visit to Miss Betsey's house.

9. Describe David's life at Mr. Strong's school.

10. Describe David's visit to Uriah Heep's and Micawber's houses.

11. Describe Mr. Micawber's Gauntlet.

12. Describe David's visit to Dora's house.

13. What change had come in the behaviour of Dr. Strong, Mrs. Strong and Mr. Micawber?

14. What achievements were adumbrated by David?

15. What ordeal with servants did David and Dora notice?

16. Explain the spat between Mr. and Mrs. Strong? How did Mr. Dick bring about reconciliation?

17. Describe Traddles' role in bringing Uriah to his knees.

18. Describe David's Sojourm abroad.

19. Describe David and Traddles' visit to the prison and Uriah's imprisonment.

20. Describe David's visit to Agnes' and his marriage with her.

21. What pieces of exciting news were given by Mr. Peggotty as he visited David and Agnes?

Long Questions

1. Give a brief description of David as told by himself.

2. Describe the role of Miss Betsey in the novel.

3. Give a character-sketch of Micawber.

4. Give a character-sketch of Peggotty.

5. Describe David's relationships with Agnes, Dora and Clara.

6. Explain the role of Emily in the novel.

7. Explain the villainy of Uriah Heep.

8. Describe David's various friends.

9. Explain the role of the Mr. Spenlow and Mr. Jorkins.

❑❑❑

Printed in the USA
CPSIA information can be obtained
at www.ICGtesting.com
LVHW021055170724
785764LV00007B/358